IF WAR IS NOTHING MORE THAN LISTS OF BATTLES
THEN HUMAN LIVES COUNT LESS THAN SABER RATTLES

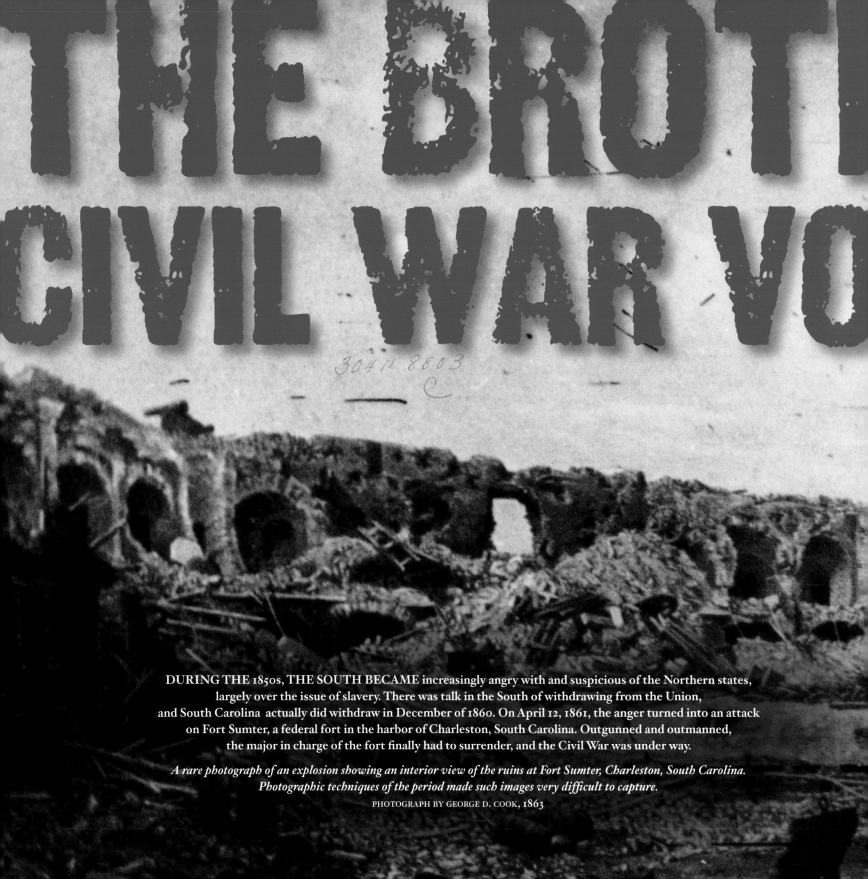

THE BROT

CIVIL WAR VO

DURING THE 1850s, THE SOUTH BECAME increasingly angry with and suspicious of the Northern states, largely over the issue of slavery. There was talk in the South of withdrawing from the Union, and South Carolina actually did withdraw in December of 1860. On April 12, 1861, the anger turned into an attack on Fort Sumter, a federal fort in the harbor of Charleston, South Carolina. Outgunned and outmanned, the major in charge of the fort finally had to surrender, and the Civil War was under way.

A rare photograph of an explosion showing an interior view of the ruins at Fort Sumter, Charleston, South Carolina. Photographic techniques of the period made such images very difficult to capture.

PHOTOGRAPH BY GEORGE D. COOK, 1863

IERS' WAR
CES IN VERSE

BY J. PATRICK LEWIS
INCLUDING PHOTOGRAPHS BY CIVIL WAR PHOTOGRAPHERS

NATIONAL GEOGRAPHIC
WASHINGTON, D.C.

CONTENTS

ALTHOUGH THE NORTH COMMANDED a federal army, most of the Southern officers and soldiers resigned
and returned to their states to fight for the Confederacy, against the men with whom they had so recently served side by side.
Existing state militias joined the side their states were on, and volunteers in every state poured in to form new regiments.
No one, in the North or the South, had the slightest idea of how ferocious the war would be.

Left: Eager recruits in Virginia prepare for war after their state joins the Confederacy on May 23, 1861.
PHOTOGRAPHER UNKNOWN

INTRODUCTION

The numbers are so staggering that they stop meaning anything. Two hundred sixty thousand dead for the Confederacy. Three hundred and sixty thousand dead for the Union. And those are the conservative estimates; we do not really know how many soldiers died, certainly not the number of civilians. Hundreds of thousands more men were wounded. Numbers, numbers. They eclipse the people themselves.

But the Civil War involved real people, of course. Real people who lived real lives and made real decisions that mattered. Some of them affected the very outcome of the war.

Still, the numbers matter. So many men mobilized, North and South. So many that no one, North or South, went untouched. Farmers—or the wives they left behind— had a hard time finding help to plant the crops in the spring and harvest them in the fall. In some towns, so many men of military age were gone that the young women had no one to court them.

Most importantly, everyone knew someone in the war, and nearly everyone knew someone who died in it. By the end of the war, loss shrouded both sides. And then there was the last and most notable casualty of this war: Abraham Lincoln, the man who had held the Union together almost by sheer force of will.

These poems help capture the spirit of those Americans who lived through this awful time. Read on.

— Jennifer L. Weber
Assistant Professor, University of Kansas

THE BLOODIEST DAY OF THE CIVIL WAR occurred at Antietam, Maryland, on September 17, 1862. When the one-day battle ended, 10,000 Confederate and 12,000 Union troops were dead, wounded, or missing.

Left: Dead soldiers lie near the Dunker Church at Antietam, Maryland.
PHOTOGRAPH BY ALEXANDER GARDNER, 1862

DOWN ON THE PLANTATION

★

Picking Cotton near Savannah, Georgia

EARLY 1860s

I stopped to stoop
And stooped to chop,
Then clipped to scoop
The cotton crop.

The way it went
Long after dark...
A woman bent
Like a question mark.

COTTON WAS BY FAR THE MOST IMPORTANT CROP of the South. By 1860, cotton production had grown to 4.5 million bales a year (a bale weighed 500 pounds), and cotton made up more than one-half of all U.S. exports. Slaves made such production, and its profits, possible. Planting and picking cotton was a year-round job. Preparing the fields and planting the cotton began in January and ended in June. By that time, the first cotton bolls were ready for picking. An adult slave was expected to pick about 120 pounds of cotton a day. Picking ended just before Christmas.

Left: When it was time to pick cotton, everyone went to work—men, women, and any child old enough to help.
This group stopped the back-breaking work to have a photograph taken.

PHOTOGRAPHER UNKNOWN

JOHN BROWN HATED SLAVERY and worked to abolish it all his life. His dream was to gather a force of abolitionists to invade the South, believing that slaves would join them and rise up against their masters. He began with an audacious scheme to take over the federal armory and all its weapons at Harper's Ferry, Virginia, then arm the slaves and start the revolution. He failed and was jailed, tried, and hanged for his crimes.

Harper's Ferry, showing the destruction from an 1865 battle in which the armory and several buildings, shown in the lower left-hand corner, were destroyed.
PHOTOGRAPH BY JAMES AND ALEXANDER GARDNER, JULY 1865

THE RAIDER

★

John Brown at Harper's Ferry, Virginia
OCTOBER 16, 1859

Against a barbarous slave trade,
I swore with my last breath
Twenty-one worthies, black and white
And unafraid of death,

Would take the Armory that night.
We fought outmanned, outgunned,
And could not hold the prize though we
Had permanently stunned

Savage bigots everywhere.
We swung for it, but Lee,
That vile coward, must accept
Responsibility.

Let all the hired guns of hate
Punish this old John Brown.
The dam they opened up will flood
With blood until they drown.

In truth I am a white man,
In sympathy a black.
But for this rope, I might have seen
Us win our freedom back.

BLOOD OF OUR FATHERS, BLOOD OF OUR SONS

★

The First Battle of Bull Run

JULY 21, 1861

Five thousand fell that day by Sudley Road,

Five thousand left their mothers in despair.

A world gone red—the Bull Run overflowed

With blood, raining in the violent air.

On Widow Henry's fallow fields, I saw

A boy about my age fall where he stood,

Face down, writhing, clutching at mud and straw,

As if God's earth could do him any good.

By what outrageous powers of circumstance

Do men take arms against their very own?

The Yankee sergeant's bullet snapped the bone.

Roy Pugh, his Rebel son, had little chance.

Distraught, the sergeant rolled him on his side.

Roy whispered, "Father…Why?" before he died.

FROM THE VERY BEGINNING, the fever of war found members of the same family passionately supporting opposing views and even facing each other on battlefields. The First Battle of Bull Run was a Confederate victory, though the rebels were too fatigued and disorganized to pursue the Union army. Some 4,700 men were killed, wounded, or captured.

Left: This Confederate infantryman's youth was typical of many who joined the armies—and who too often never saw home again.

PHOTOGRAPH BY ALEXANDER GARDNER

BOYS IN A BROTHERS' WAR

Near Richmond, Virginia

MAY 31, 1862

In the bloody Battle of Seven Pines,
a young soldier, Absalom Flowers,
whose mother baked the most delicious cobbler
in Roanoke, whose father was nothing really,
stopped a Union bullet with his face. Rolling slowly
downhill, he concluded on the home of a vole.
A sprawling monument to insanity.

Ignorant of war, the vole had his pea-sized heart
set on the bark of a chinaberry tree, but there
was Private Flowers' boot. The vole's wife
scampered along the tunnel to sniff the unwanted
guest. Through the crack, she could see only darkness
in the Seven Pines sky.

The wind shifted, and moaned as it should.
Hobart Funderburk, nineteen, three months married,
one month lost, screaming in another world,
felt in his stomach the welcome ice of bayonet.
Miles later, at the voles' threshold, Hobart rolled hard
into Absalom.

In this way the sickle moon was revealed.

THE BATTLE OF SEVEN PINES was an exercise in calamities. One Confederate general inadvertently led his troops down
the wrong road and away from the battle. Another Confederate general had his men march in columns, but out of sight of one another,
which ruled out a coordinated attack. New Union recruits fled in disarray when the fighting began.
The chaotic battle ended with terrible losses—almost 8,000 Confederate and nearly 5,000 Union casualties and no ground gained by anyone.
After this, General Robert E. Lee was made commander of the Army of Northern Virginia

Streams and fords played a major part in Civil War battles in Virginia. Here, at Sudley Springs, Union forces found
a place to cross the stream and were able to attack Confederate troops at Seven Pines.
PHOTOGRAPHER UNKNOWN

I AM FAST IN MY CHAINS

Frederick Douglass
Abolitionist

Down where the slaves lie broken
    Under a slant-wind sky,
The sleepy land heard spoken
    Words to electrify.

Bleak history of two nations,
    My own slave narrative
Told what the white plantations
    Took but refused to give.

In war's pathetic season,
    I bid my brothers, "Go
Get at the throat of treason"
    And lay the traitors low.

Let that voice never weaken
    That summons people's pride.
Let it be freedom's beacon
    Across the long divide.

FREDERICK DOUGLASS once told an audience, "I appear this evening as a thief and robber. I stole this head, these limbs, this body from my master, and ran off with them." He proved so eloquent a speaker that many could not believe he had been a slave. In 1845 he published *Narrative of the Life of Frederick Douglass, An American Slave*.

Left: Frederick Douglass, famed abolitionist and former slave

PHOTOGRAPHER UNKNOWN

NATHANIEL GWINNETT— SHRAPNEL WOUND

Battle of Antietam
SEPTEMBER 17, 1862

My head no longer held
A thought without a doubt.
This ragged heart had swelled,
The fire was burning out.

I loved to trade on talk
But never heard the words.
They let me out to walk—
I'd fly among the birds.

My brothers rode to war
Into Confederate flak,
Their wives had known before
They'd not be riding back.

And I, who loved love most
With every fractured breath,
Was giving up the ghost
To welcome Mr. Death.

Gathering up my things,
And very like a loon
On agitated wings,
I flew against the moon.

CIVIL WAR DOCTORS did their best to save sick and wounded soldiers, but their knowledge of disease and infection was very limited. They were unaware that germs caused disease, that they could be passed from person to person, or that they thrived in unsanitary conditions. Nor did doctors know about antiseptics, which could sterilize surgical instruments, plates, cups—almost anything that touched a sick or wounded soldier.

Right: A nurse tends the wounded in a Union hospital in Nashville, Tennessee.
PHOTOGRAPHER UNKNOWN

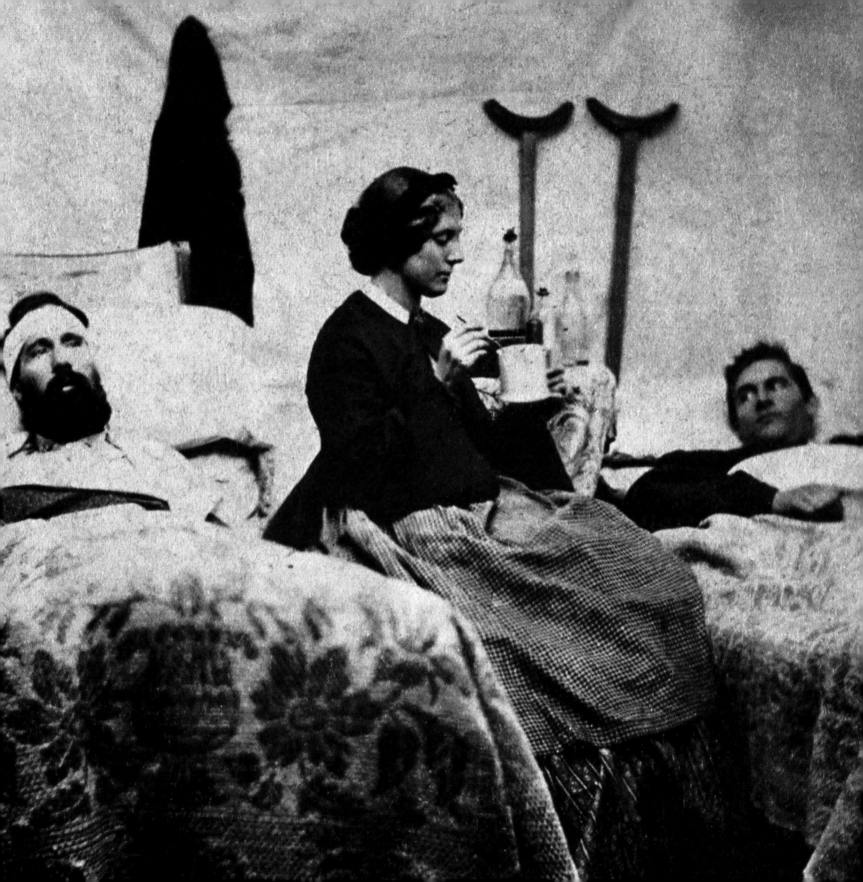

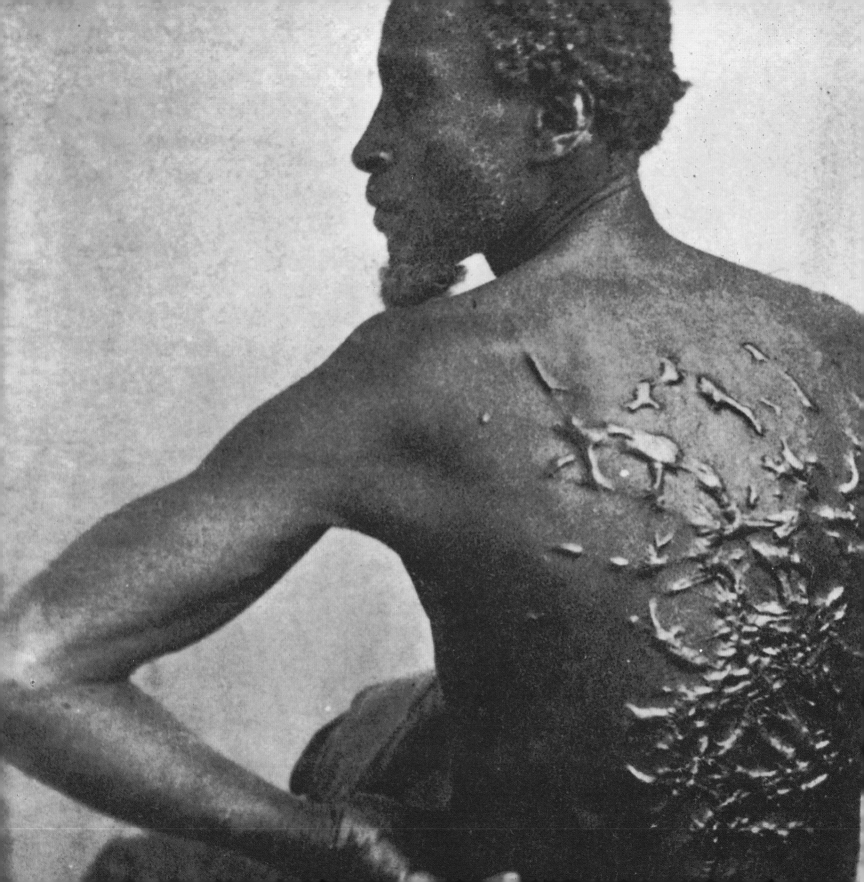

WHITE NIGHTMARE

★

Runaway Slave, Milledgeville, Georgia

AUGUST 1863

Cracked jackets of field corn bake
At the back end of Heartbreak, Georgia.
Easing my way north through the yellowing
Tallboys, I'm Solomon "Black" Jacks,
On the cliff of nineteen, on the run
From shackles and fear, stopping to hear
The lies late August tells. A blue racer
Coils at my feet. Swifts hurricane the nest
Of my dust-downed hair. An orphan cloud
Stalls like a thought. I dream-sail the gray
Nimbus past the whole thin shimmer
Of my come-to-nothing life—
The gaunt captain of a ship called
Consequence on a day named Desire—
Hunched down on the sun-spidered tile
Of Georgia looking back looking ahead
Wondering whether I can ride out
Of this white nightmare on the back of a five
Dollar bill and bullwhip-long odds
Of making it in a land as alien as space
And altogether improbable as Pennsylvania.

BEFORE THE WAR, a slave escaping Georgia had to travel more than 1,000 miles to freedom. Few succeeded. By 1863 however, Union troops had penetrated far into the South. Escaping was still dangerous, but the trip to Union camps was far shorter. Though escaping slaves of this period perhaps dreamed of a new life in the North, many wound up working for the Union Army and remaining in the South after the war.

Left: The scarred back of a slave shows how severely he was whipped.

PHOTOGRAPHER UNKNOWN

LETTER FROM HOME

★

Written from Fountain Spring, West Virginia
MAY 1864

Dear James,
Yr ma, God help her, swore at Bible groups
Her boy'd be home before the swallows dare.
But then, at Spotsylvania, Yankee troops
Put Horse and Boot to that cussed affair.
Nigh on two months of rumers, son. We heard
They's 30,000 (?) men lade down to die.
Yr ma's plumb worried sick her solem word
Her boy is safe and hedin' home's a lie.
And now they say our neibor Jacob Todd—
Remember him? Rode two campains with Lee.
A shell blew half his body back to God.
His brother Roy, Corporal, Artillery,
Knelt down in Jacob's blood and vissera
And shut his lifeliss eyes.

Come home,
Yr Pa

LETTER HOME

★

Written on the road to a Union Prison for Confederate Prisoners of War

AUGUST 1864

Dear Pa,
We's bent on losin' independence, yessir.
I'm Over Joyed with battels rebbies won,
But God by God takes up with our opresser
Like boysinberrys sup on noonday sun.
They shot my horse from under me. I bled
Buckits into Virginee's killing ground,
A Minie bullet lodjed upside my head.
I've no idea xackly where I'm bound.
Tell ma the Union food ain't bad (its worse!)—
Rank bacon, peas and sea crackers. The guns
Are murder, but diseas rides its own hearse.
This war thins mothers' sons to skeletons.
But hold on, Pa, read them survivors names.
I aim to be among 'em,

Yr son,
James

CORRESPONDENCE DURING THE WAR traveled slowly, as these letters show.
The son has become a Union prisoner as his father urges him to come home. Both sides took prisoners
and set up camps to hold them. The most notorious was the Confederate stockade of Andersonville,
in southwest Georgia. Nearly 13,000 Union prisoners died there from dysentery, scurvy,
malaria, starvation, and exposure in the most inhumane conditions imaginable.

I CAN MAKE GEORGIA HOWL

★

William Tecumseh Sherman on his March to the Sea

NOVEMBER 15–DECEMBER 21, 1864

From Atlanta to Savannah
In a winter month or more
Was a march called devastation
Like they'd never seen before.

They called it a destruction
Razed by sixty-thousand blues
To the city of Savannah—
Righteousness's wrecking crews.

Though my tactics were in question,
And I mapped a rugged route,
No one second-guessed the outcome
'Cause it never was in doubt.

Oh, we robbed and burned and pillaged
As we gathered what we must
For the journey to the water
And we left behind disgust.

So Savannah was a Christmas gift
To Lincoln, thanks to me,
And a nail in the coffin of
Surrender, General Lee.

UNION GENERAL WILLIAM TECUMSEH SHERMAN started his March to the Sea from Atlanta, Georgia.
He took every town he came to, leaving a swath of destruction behind. At his order, his troops destroyed anything that could
be of use to Confederate troops—roads, bridges, railroads, buildings, livestock, and crops.
After reaching the sea at Savannah, he turned north and continued through South and North Carolina.

*Left: All along his route, General Sherman made sure his troops destroyed the railroad, the one artery for food and supplies for the South.
To be certain the tracks could not be used again, the men built bonfires from railroad ties, stuck the rails into the flames,
then bent the red-hot rails around trees, thus creating "Sherman's neckties."*

PHOTOGRAPH BY GEORGE N. BARNARD, 1864

PASSING IN REVIEW

The tortured howls,
The wretched noise,
The lives it dooms or redeploys . . .
A civil war breaks men from boys.

Surprise attacks—
Again, again!
Such eerie stillness now and then
Is when a war churns boys to men.

Remember them
Today, deceased,
Young men-at-arms who would increase
By inches some foothold on peace.

Salute the boys
You never knew
For valor. It's long overdue.
Young men still passing in review

Do not require
A great parade,
A big brass band or cavalcade
To sing the sacrifice they made.

THE WAR WAS OVER, but the losses were so great that they staggered the nation. Not only had hundreds of thousands died, but hundreds of thousands more returned home no longer whole.

Ironically, these amputees were the lucky ones. In a time before sterile surgery or antibiotics, most soldiers with head or abdominal injuries died. But Civil War doctors perfected the art of amputating damaged arms, legs, hands, and feet to stop the spread of infection from wounds into the bloodstream.

For the rest of their lives, these brave men stood as living reminders of the nation's sacrifices.

Right: A man with both arms amputated poses for a photograph.
PHOTOGRAPHER UNKNOWN

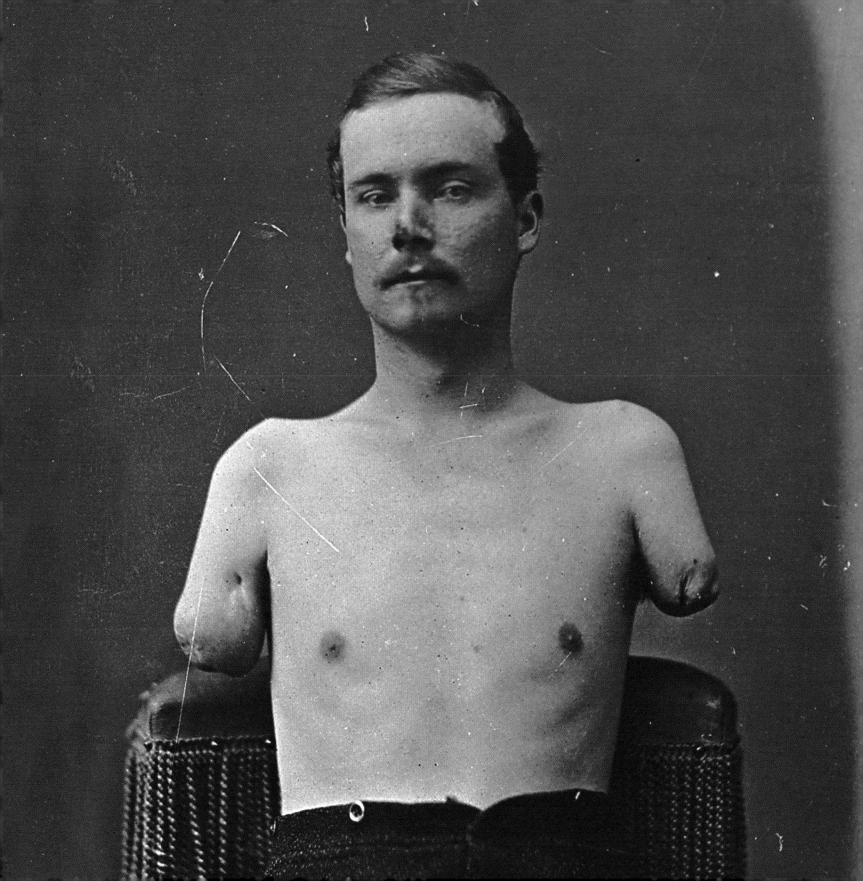

THE UNITED STATES CIVIL WAR
1861–1865

WASHINGTON TERRITORY

OREGON

DAKOTA TERRITORY

MINN.

WIS.

MICHIGAN

ME.

VT.

N.H.

N.Y.

MASS.

CONN. R.I.

NEVADA TERR.

UTAH TERRITORY

NEBRASKA TERRITORY

IOWA

ILL.

IND.

OHIO

PA.

ANTIETAM (SHARPSBURG) Sept. 17, 1862

GETTYSBURG N.J. July 1-3, 1863

CALIFORNIA

COLORADO TERRITORY

KANSAS

MO.

FIRST AND SECOND BULL RUN (MANASSAS) July 21, 1861; Aug. 29-30, 1862

MD. DEL.

FREDERICKSBURG Dec. 13, 1862

WILDERNESS May 5-6, 1864

VA.

COLD HARBOR June 1-3, 1864

PUBLIC LAND STRIP

NEW MEXICO TERRITORY

UNORGANIZED TERRITORY

Boundary of Confederate States

KY.

APPOMATTOX COURT HOUSE Apr. 9, 1865

N.C.

SIEGE OF PETERSBURG mid June 1864- early Apr. 1865

TENN.

SHILOH Apr. 6-7, 1862

CHICKAMAUGA Sept. 19-20, 1863

CHANCELLORSVILLE May 1-4, 1863

ARK.

S.C.

ATLANTA July 22, 1864

FT. SUMTER Apr. 12-13, 1861

MISS.

ALA.

GA.

SIEGE OF VICKSBURG May 18-July 4, 1863

CHATTANOOGA Nov. 23-25, 1863

TEXAS

LA.

FLA.

NEW ORLEANS Apr. 25-May 1, 1862

Legend
- ⚜ Selected major battle
- — Boundary of Confederate States
- ▨ Slave states that seceded
- ▨ Slave states and regions remaining in the Union
- ▨ Free states
- ▨ United States territories

miles 0 — 400
km 0 — 600

Boundaries represent late 1861.

▬ TIME LINE OF SELECTED EVENTS FROM THE CIVIL WAR ▬

The dates in the top section refer to events in the poems and notes. The lower section guides you through other key moments of the War.

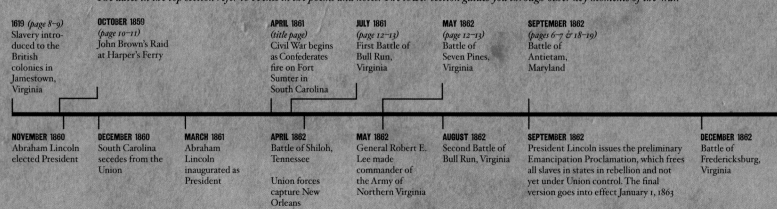

1619 *(page 8–9)*
Slavery introduced to the British colonies in Jamestown, Virginia

OCTOBER 1859 *(page 10–11)*
John Brown's Raid at Harper's Ferry

APRIL 1861 *(title page)*
Civil War begins as Confederates fire on Fort Sumter in South Carolina

JULY 1861 *(page 12–13)*
First Battle of Bull Run, Virginia

MAY 1862 *(page 12–13)*
Battle of Seven Pines, Virginia

SEPTEMBER 1862 *(pages 6–7 & 18–19)*
Battle of Antietam, Maryland

NOVEMBER 1860
Abraham Lincoln elected President

DECEMBER 1860
South Carolina secedes from the Union

MARCH 1861
Abraham Lincoln inaugurated as President

APRIL 1862
Battle of Shiloh, Tennessee

Union forces capture New Orleans

MAY 1862
General Robert E. Lee made commander of the Army of Northern Virginia

AUGUST 1862
Second Battle of Bull Run, Virginia

SEPTEMBER 1862
President Lincoln issues the preliminary Emancipation Proclamation, which frees all slaves in states in rebellion and not yet under Union control. The final version goes into effect January 1, 1863

DECEMBER 1862
Battle of Fredericksburg, Virginia

A NOTE ON THE PHOTOGRAPHY

IN 1861, the Civil War had just begun and Matthew Brady, an established photographer with studios in New York and Washington, decided that the war needed to be visually documented in a body of work that would comprise a "portrait of the war." Known for his studio photography of famous people, including presidents and visiting royalty, Brady hired teams of photographers and sent them into the field.

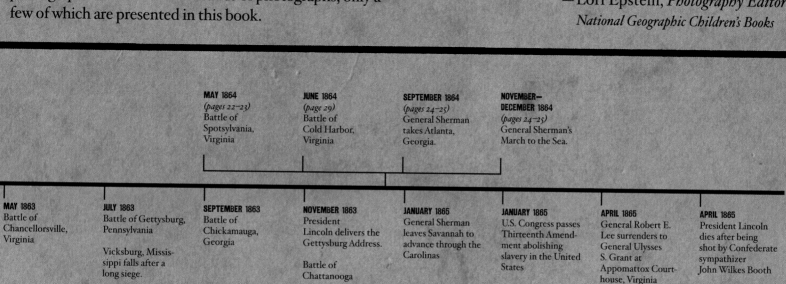

The photographers traveled in pairs, driving canopy-covered, horse-drawn wagons filled with enough chemicals and glass plates to photograph and develop pictures for weeks at a time. Photographers Alexander Gardner and Timothy O'Sullivan began working for Brady but then left him to set up similar studios. Photographs were often credited to the studio and not the actual photographer. By the end of the war, these studios and their photographers had taken thousands of photographs, only a few of which are presented in this book.

Capturing these images was no easy task. The cameras were big and had to be mounted atop tripods to hold them up. Large, heavy pieces of glass were smeared with wet, toxic chemicals and placed in the camera to be exposed to light. The lens cap was removed for 5 to 30 seconds, depending on the available sunlight. The subject had to sit very still, otherwise the image would blur. If a person blinked or swayed a little, the image came out looking like there was a ghost in the picture! That is why there are so few images of actual battle, or other action, during the Civil War.

If you'd like to see more Civil War photographs, visit The Library of Congress at www.loc.gov or The National Archives and Records Administration at www.nara.gov.

— Lori Epstein, *Photography Editor*
National Geographic Children's Books

MAY 1864
(pages 22–23)
Battle of Spotsylvania, Virginia

JUNE 1864
(page 29)
Battle of Cold Harbor, Virginia

SEPTEMBER 1864
(pages 24–25)
General Sherman takes Atlanta, Georgia.

NOVEMBER– DECEMBER 1864
(pages 24–25)
General Sherman's March to the Sea.

MAY 1863
Battle of Chancellorsville, Virginia

JULY 1863
Battle of Gettysburg, Pennsylvania

Vicksburg, Mississippi falls after a long siege.

SEPTEMBER 1863
Battle of Chickamauga, Georgia

NOVEMBER 1863
President Lincoln delivers the Gettysburg Address.

Battle of Chattanooga

JANUARY 1865
General Sherman leaves Savannah to advance through the Carolinas

JANUARY 1865
U.S. Congress passes Thirteenth Amendment abolishing slavery in the United States

APRIL 1865
General Robert E. Lee surrenders to General Ulysses S. Grant at Appomattox Courthouse, Virginia

APRIL 1865
President Lincoln dies after being shot by Confederate sympathizer John Wilkes Booth

AUTHOR'S NOTES ON POEMS

The Civil War (1861–1865) left a scar on the American psyche that resulted in millions of words and hundreds of books that analyze and commemorate the conflict. This book is a modest addition to the whole. But rather than tell about battles and generals and politics, this collection offers glimpses of the war experience, especially its emotional side.

In writing the poems, I tried to create an homage to those who lived through that experience or died from it. I wanted to evoke their voices—blue and gray, victorious and defeated, black and white, exalted and misguided.

War may seem an odd subject for poetry, but there is nothing in this world or out of it that does not bend to the poetic. The stuff of poetry is in the daily news and in daily clues to the ordinary. Your pocket is a country; your garden, a continent; your book, a ticket to ride.

To prepare for the challenge, I explored this time of dread wonder through dozens of books and articles, and I scoured the internet for diary entries and first-hand accounts.

I wanted to create a palpable sense of what it must have been like to be there, both as a participant and as a mute witness to the muttering cycle of death, the hundreds of thousands of young lives stopped by cannon or volley or the folly of determined generals.

Now, reader, you become the writer. I hope that when you read these poems you will be encouraged to try your own hand at a poem written from a point of view not your own. Use any style or form that expresses the voice of the person you are trying to bring to life. Then write another, telling the same story from another point of view. Every event can be seen through multiple prisms.

DOWN ON THE PLANTATION
I wondered how it would be possible to capture the absolute horror of slavery in a very short poem. After all, volumes have been written about this "peculiar institution," as southern whites once called it. I wanted to create a single image that would evoke in the reader a moment of understanding, something to think about long after the poem was put away.

THE RAIDER
How many people have been as committed to a cause—the abolition of slavery, in his case—as John Brown? I could not leave him out of this account any more than I could ignore Frederick Douglass, who said of Brown, "in truth he is a white man, in sympathy a black man," a line I use in the poem. John Brown is a complex figure—an abolitionist leader who felt that the end of slavery would only be achieved through violent revolution. Because I wrote the poem in Brown's voice from beyond the grave, the emphasis is on his strong belief that even though he had failed to carry out his plan, blood would soon flow over the issue of slavery.

BLOOD OF OUR FATHERS, BLOOD OF OUR SONS
Though the names here are fictional, battlefield instances of father and son fighting on opposite sides did occur. Captain D. P. Conyngham, an officer in the Irish Brigade, described one such tragedy at http://www.eyewitnesstohistory.com/malvern.htm.

BOYS IN A BROTHER'S WAR
Here is an example of an imaginary event that for me grew more real in the telling. Did animals who lived on the battlefields—such as the voles in the poem—experience the war as if they were civilian bystanders? Not likely. What can't be doubted, though, is that we human bystanders to war—past and present—are often blind to the shocking events taking place all around us, distracted by our own small concerns.

I AM FAST IN MY CHAINS
Frederick Douglass's slave narrative is one of the most powerful political documents ever written and the inspiration for my poem. The rhythmic and rhyming form seemed to have just the right flavor to evoke Douglass's voice.

NATHANIEL GWINNETT— SHRAPNEL WOUND

Nathaniel Gwinnett is a figment of my imagination, but a man-boy by another name, far from home, surely endured similar experiences as death approached. Sound is every bit as important as sense in a poem. The insistent rhymes of this poem sound a drum beat that suggests the inevitable approach of death. On a personal note, this form resonates deeply with me because it uses the same tone and tenor as I used in a poem I wrote for my dying father.

WHITE NIGHTMARE

Again, this poem began with wondering. I wondered how a young slave who dared to run for his life might have seen himself in the midst of that endeavor. How many Solomon "Black" Jacks were there? Was the risk worth it? I imagined myself a man, humbled by birth and consequences, determined though fearful to escape, desperate and courageous. For this poem—about seeking freedom—what could I use but free verse?

LETTER FROM HOME and LETTER HOME

These sonnets were inspired by hundreds of letters written by Civil War soldiers and their loved ones. I wanted to convey a sense of a father's unease and a son's plight, the two men bound together in fear and despair. I'm not sure why these poems came to me as sonnets, but it never occurred to me to write them in any other form.

I CAN MAKE GEORGIA HOWL

General Sherman meant to win the war for the Union whatever it took, and he was proud of his fierce and violent methods. The ballad seemed a good form for this warrior happy to brag about his grim success. For more information, see http://www.shermansrevenge.com/. And for a Southerner's viewpoint, see http://eyewitnesstohistory.com/sherman.htm.

PASSING IN REVIEW

I wrote this poem on Veterans' Day though it applies to any day of the year. I chose a form in which the repetition gives a sound-sense of marching.

BIBLIOGRAPHY

Civil War author and expert James M. McPherson estimates that there are some 50,000 volumes on the subject. Here is a sample of books for the Civil War beginner.

Berlin, Ira, ed. *Freedom: A Documentary History of Emancipation 1861–1867, 2 vols.* (1982).

Blair, Jayne E. *The Essential Civil War: A Handbook to the Battles, Armies, Navies and Commanders* (2006).

Bowman, John S., ed. *The Civil War Almanac* (1983).

Carter, Alice E. and Richard Jensen. *The Civil War on the Web: A Guide to the Very Best Sites, 2nd ed.* (2003).

Catton, Bruce and James M. McPherson, *American Heritage New History of the Civil War* (2001).

Commager, Henry Steele, ed. *The Blue and the Gray: The Story of the Civil War as Told by Participants* (1950).

Crane, Stephen, *The Red Badge of Courage* (1895).

Davis, William C., ed. *The Image of War 1861–1865, 6 vols.* (1984).

Doctorow, E.L., *The March* (2005).

Douglass, Frederick. *Narrative of the Life of Frederick Douglass, American Slave.* (1845)

Faust, Patricia L., ed. *Historical Times Illustrated Encyclopedia of the Civil War* (1987).

Foote, Shelby. *The Civil War: A Narrative, 3 vols.* (1958, 1963, 1974).

Long, E. B., ed. *The Civil War Day by Day* (1971).

McPherson, James M. *Battle Cry of Freedom: The Civil War Era* (1988).

_____. *Ordeal by Fire: The Civil War and Reconstruction* (1982).

Nevins, Allan. *The War for the Union, 4 vols.* (1971).

Ward, Geoffrey C. *The Civil War* (1990), based on the PBS series by Ken Burns.

Werner, Emmy E. *Reluctant Witnesses: Children's Voices from the Civil War* (1998).

Wheeler, Richard. *Voices of the Civil War* (1976).

Whitman, Walt. *Specimen Days* (1971).

_____. *Walt Whitman's Civil War.* (1989)

Wiley, Bell Irvin. *The Life of Billy Yank: The Common Soldier of the Union* (1984).

_____. *The Life of Johnny Reb: The Common Soldier of the Confederacy* (1984).

Wilson, Edmund. *Patriotic Gore: Studies in the Literature of the American Civil War* (1994).

Woodward, C. Vann, ed. *Mary Chestnut's Civil War* (1981).

For Mick, whose hand is in it all. Love, Pat

Sources for the Captions
Allen, Thomas B., *The Blue and the Gray.* Washington, D.C.: National Geographic Society, 1992.
Kagan, Neal, ed. Narrative by Stephen J. Hyslop. *Eyewitness to the Civil War: The Complete History from Secession to Reconstruction.*
Washington, D.C.: National Geographic Society, 2006.

Sources for the Photographs
LOC refers to the Library of Congress
Front cover: LOC; Back cover: LOC; Title page: LOC; p. 4, Valentine Richmond History Center; p. 6,
LOC; p. 8, Corbis; p. 10–11, LOC; p. 12, David Wynn Vaughn Collection; p. 15, LOC; p. 16, LOC; p. 18–19, U.S. Army Military History Institute;
p. 20, LOC; p. 22–23, LOC; p. 24, LOC; p. 27, LOC; p. 29 LOC.

Book design by Bea Jackson
Production assistance by Sandi Owatverot, David M. Seager, and Ruth Thompson.
Many thanks to Jennifer L. Weber, Assistant Professor, University of Kansas, for her expert review of the text and pictures.
Special thanks to Nancy Feresten, Lori Epstein, and Jo Tunstall.
Map by Carl Mehler and Matt Chwastyk.

Text for this book is set in Hoefler Text.
Display text is set in Asphaltum.

Library of Congress Cataloging-in-Publication Data
Lewis, J. Patrick.
The brothers' war : Civil War voices in verse / by J. Patrick Lewis ;
p. cm.
ISBN 978-1-4263-0036-3 (trade) — ISBN 978-1-4263-0037-0 (lib. bdg.)
1. United States—History—Civil War, 1861–1865—Poetry. I. Title.
PS3562.E9465B76 2007
811'.54—dc22

2006103275

Founded in 1888, the National Geographic Society is one of the largest nonprofit scientific and educational organizations in the world.
It reaches more than 285 million people worldwide each month through its official journal, NATIONAL GEOGRAPHIC, and its four
other magazines; the National Geographic Channel; television documentaries; radio programs; films; books; videos and DVDs;
maps; and interactive media. National Geographic has funded more than 8,000 scientific research projects and
supports an education program combating geographic illiteracy.

National Geographic Society
1145 17th Street N.W. • Washington, D.C. 20036-4688 • U.S.A.

Visit the Society's Web site: www.nationalgeographic.com

Printed in China

For information about special discounts for bulk purchases, please contact National Geographic Books Special Sales: ngspecsales@ngs.org.